FROM THEN UNTIL NOW
~The Net of Love~

A collection of poems
by
Donna Wandler

Donna Wandler

Krackle Group
Publishers
USA

FROM THEN UNTIL NOW
~The Net of Love~

1. Poems 2. Proving Grounds
3. Quotes 4. Growing Panes

ISBN: 978-1508985686

Sweet is the story you shall tell at eventide when day is done.

Mat 7: 24 *Whosoever heareth these sayings of mine and doeth them, I will liken him unto a wise man which built his house upon the rock.*

Mat 7:26 *Whosoever heareth these sayings of mine and doeth them not, I will liken him unto a foolish man which built his house upon the sand.*

Introduction

From Then Until Now contains much of my poetry and is being published to commemorate forty years since I first made my choice to serve God in spirit and in truth. *Proving Ground* and *Growing Panes* were the titles of two previous booklets given as gifts to family and friends. Other poems have since been added and arranged more by subject than by the date written. I have no formal training as a poet, it is just the expression my pen takes. The content comes from my heart, not my head. Ruth gleaned because of necessity and what she gathered was enough to sustain her own life and that of another. May we be willing to gather what has been left for us.

Donna Wandler

Table of Contents
(Part I)

Table of Contents
(Part II)

Deut 29:29 *The secret things belong unto the Lord our God, but those things which are revealed belong to us and to our children forever, that we may do all the words of this law*

Part I
Proving Grounds
Poems of Faith and Inspiration

The passage of time shows the process of growth, so the experiences of others can offer gleanings that feed our own meditations.

Things That Matter

All the things in life that matter
Require a conscious choice

Every step we take will ask us
What things still matter most

Sometimes the most difficult choices
Are clearer when we see

They can be viewed from here on earth
Or from eternity

And all our choices and efforts
Relate to this main theme

And prove which nature defines us
By how we choose to see

There is a Light

Is there a light that shines today
Through this worlds gloom and blight

A light much like one long ago
That wise men sought at night

A light that still illuminates
God's way and truth and life

That shows again his son anew
The life that God delights

Is there a light still shining on
A homeless stable scene

A simple, lowly way of life
Where new life within remains

Is the focus of the light still on
The Christ, the son of God

For men still seek him as he was
In ways now dim and marred

Do the wise still search at any cost
To find the King of kings

He is the treasure hid, not lost
His presence still remains

His Spirit, Life and Word still light
A song the shepherds sing

He is the light of this dark world
Eternal it remains

Each Day

Each day the earth turns

Completely around

To fit into the plan of God

The sun and moon

Remain set in their course

The stars fixed in place by his word

All creation gives voice to his glory

His handiwork praises his name

As a witness to all generations

God is here!

God is still the same!

Proving Ground

A handful of earth I'd give to you
    Just some soil from the ground today
To cast upon a seed of worth
    That lies within the clay

I cannot give you all the things
    That are within your reach
I can only share what's mine to give
    The things beneath my feet

For all the steps I've taken
    Along life's journey too
Have taught me all the things to keep
    Of what is good and true

In every harsh experience
    That shows our frailty
God wants to teach us by his grace
    What is reality

He would show us all the things of time
That are snares along the way
That take our time and talents
When no profit will they pay

And living on the edge of things
Won't keep the harm away
When we seek to please ourselves
The pleasures rarely last a day

For all the victories we would claim
The marks we would possess
Must be fought along the borders
Of our inheritance

Now I trust in each experience
The hand held out to me
And take the gifts that He would give
To keep me from defeat

For God who is far wiser
Than man could ever be
Said, "The proving ground you're walking on
Is hallowed ground to me"

You are Caught in the Net of His Love
(Matt.4:18-19)

Seeking and wandering alone in the night
Sighing and crying and searching for light

Reading and praying and waiting to hear
Words bringing comfort, my heart to cheer

Asking and longing for hope not in vain
Fearful yet knocking, I pressed on again

Then two who were seeking a lost soul to find
Spoke words of assurance to this heart of mine

Questions were answered from lives full of peace
A wonderful message caused my struggle to cease

Eden

There were choices in the garden
    Choices still for us today
Will we find the needed answers
    Will it prompt us all to pray

For by ourselves we soon will fail
    In choosing only good
Life seems so mixed with right and wrong
    To discern it as we should

For we are only a step away
    From doing good or ill
And influencing others by our choice
    That time will only seal

God would help us in this matter
    For he longs that we might know
His provision made in Jesus
    And the love he wants to show

He would teach us all his judgments
    And the way that he has planned
For he leads in ways of mercies
    That are ever near at hand

And he longs that we might see the end
    Of taking our own way
To see the Christ on Calvary's cross
    Our cup of woe to pay

Let it prompt us now to listen
    To the voice that's from on high
Draw us closer to his presence
    Know salvation's gift that's nigh

Doubt

Is like a drip
That slips into cracks of hardness
Constantly reminding us of the flaws
Within ourselves and others
It's a distraction with lesser things
That fill our time
And plague our hearts
It's a whispered thought
Contrary, yet slightly believable
That like a wedge
Can force a gap between
Our faith
And
Our hope
Paralyzing us and destroying
Our willingness and purpose

Hope

Is a song in the night
A comfort in distress
A present sacrifice
A future reward
It is looking beyond the immediate
It is a strong, clear thought or
Vision of what *could* be
It is the right hand of faith
And is fed by the river of life
It is lofty, noble and full of virtue
Binding the desires
And thoughts of the soul
To that which is within the heart of God

There is a Voice

There is a voice that speaks to me so clearly every day
It causes me to stop and think what I might do or say

"I need a life to dwell within: who will give their life I pray?
To show the world a saving grace, that's meant for them today"

"I need two hands to do the work, a willing heart proved true
And feet to follow by my side, the better way to do"

"I need a voice; who'll be a voice, no need for place or care
A still small voice that echoes words of comfort, hope and cheer"

It draws with loving kindness and speaks so graciously
And cares about the little things most folks forget to be

This voice I hear I'll not forget, it's proven to be true
Though skies are bright or overcast, I'll yield my life to you

I noticed a wonderful connection between Gen.24 and John 4. We see the attributes of the chosen bride in Genesis and in John we see the reality of her beginnings. What a wonderful picture of redemption and salvation. She sings *"I never can forget the day the lowly Saviour came my way"*

In the Beginning

An unlikely story yet precious and true
　　How Jesus found us, spoke to me and to you

It began when our journey led to a well
　　While seeking again our own vessel to fill

It began being drawn to hear Jesus word
　　It began when his voice to our heart was heard

It began when our thirst acknowledged truth
　　It began when our spirit accepted it too

It began when we recognized Jesus as Lord
　　It began when he revealed himself through his word

It began when we realized we were in error
　　It begins when we trust in Christ and know his care

It begins when we leave behind old ways for new
　　It begins with the good news of all Christ can do

Deep Calleth unto Deep

Beyond the ebb and flow of life
　　Uncharted paths remain
Within the current storms and cares
　　Are deeper needs unclaimed

And like the tide that washes clear
　　The sand upon the shore
Weightier issues are erased
　　And thought upon no more

Yet still they flood the memory
　　As empty feelings do
When deeper needs again arise
　　From depths we scarcely knew

Deep calleth still unto the deep
　　It hears the heart's deep cry
It calls to wake the soul again
　　Of what we oft deny

The Deep that calleth unto deep
　　Shines a light down from above
It reveals things hid in darkness
　　It reveals God's heart of love

The deep reveals the tests of time
  Reveals the worth of things
The light reveals what's buried there
  And the benefit it brings

The depth reveals how great the cost
  To remove what's hid within
The light reveals the son of God
  Who died our soul to win

God reaches to the very depths
  He calls again, again!
The deep acknowledges our loss
  And our great need of him

The Light of Life reveals God's way
  Reveals the help of heaven
God's light will draw us to his side
  When our life to him is given

Beneath the ebb and flow of life
  The heart's deep needs descend
Deep calleth yet unto the deep
  To save the souls of men

The Sons of Thunder

Revelation 10

A mighty angel comes from God
With a message for all to hear
Whose feet are planted in a way
That mortal man might fear

A rainbow is around his head
An open book in hand
A sign and seal of the eternal God
And his promises to man

The voice of him that speaketh
Are words from God's own throne
And in the days he sounds the cry
The seven thunders boom

No language bars the sound of them
No nation hides from view
Each voice re-echoes in its place
Of what was said in Truth

Sounding forth in daytime
Or in the darkest night
And everywhere their voice is heard
The message is alike

And mighty is the sound of it
And glorious is its day
When all creation hears the words
And heeds without delay

Jericho

Luke 19:1 *And Jesus entered and passed through Jericho*

A fragrant place, a lovely spot
Beside the Jordan River
With walls to keep things as they were
Lest fearful things might enter

So they shut God out and his people too
Because it threatened the only life they knew

But faithful to his least command
God's servants walked about the land
And from their lips there sounded forth
The glory of the Lord

And following faithfully day by day
A quiet people traveled on
And round about the walls they trod
Until a visible pathway formed

Then one day a shout was heard
From all God's host and heralders
For victory when the walls came down
And because a child of God was found

A fragrant place, a lovely spot
Where Jesus now can enter
A place where lost souls still are sought
Beside the Jordan River

The Net of Love

There was no bait
No lure was used
The various devices
Of men were refused

But a net was cast
In a long forgotten way
By fishers who toil
In the same way today

Casting God's net
Wherever they go
His love lights the path
As their lives they sow

Gathering, conveying
The harvest to shore
Separated, dying
To live evermore

***

Mark 1:16-20
Matt. 13:47-48

16

A banquet is not common fare.
Hearing the gospel story is without
exception the highest privilege.

The Song of Solomon
Saw Ye Him Whom My Soul Loveth?

Where comes this fragrant atmosphere
the sweet perfume that lingers still

It comes from mountaintop and hill
With prayers and sacrifice of will
It's where the treasures gathered in
And distant lands are seen again

Where comes these pleasant fruits and
spice that scent and savor rich delights

They're gleaned from fields within the gate
And some from valleys are conveyed
While others protected by garden walls
Are shared each season by one and all

Where comes this wine that speaks of death
yet lifts the soul in thankfulness

It was his feet and hands and side
That cleansed from guilt and shame his bride
And brought her forth into the light
To wear this costly garment white

Where comes this song transporting me
to see things as I'll one day see

It is the promise heaven brings
To share God's kingdom and its King
It is the song still sung today
By shepherds found within his way

The Well of Him That Liveth and Seeth Me
(The Bridegroom ~ Gen.24:65)

He came by the way of the well Lahai-roi
 To a field at the close of day

All the desires of his heart, the journey, the wait
 From his lips, no words could convey

But guided was he by a whispered thought
 That stilled all his inward care

And renewed his faith in a loving God
 Who communed with him in prayer

It caused him to lift his eyes to see
 All that he soon would behold

The servants returning faithfully
 With the bride, of whom he'd been told

The Song Of Songs

Let me recount how the gospel came, how Jesus was revealed to me
How I tasted of his love and mercy, of hope and of faith begotten
How I was taught, questions answered, needs met
Let me tell you of my search for truth, of what I found
Compare it only with the very best

Listen and I will speak of true peace and rest
Of things which I heard from on high
Listen and I will tell of things that were once hidden
And are now revealed, of how I came from a dead past
And received new life

Come and I will show you where my help sprang forth
I will tell of those who loved my soul in his stead
Who caused me to love that which He had given to them
Come and I will show you costly gifts that were freely given
Be still and hear words that direct your steps into the path of life

Come let your heart be established and your feet firmly planted
Come and hear those whom he has sent
They will show the beauties of his kingdom
Come and see what wise choices will bring. Come and find hope
Open your heart to the things which you hear

Let truth enter into your soul and hide not from it
Let your love be where it will find rest. Come and understand
More about Jesus. Seek Him in quietness and prayer
Know the unity of fellowship; see the bride in her beauty
Draw near and be encouraged; receive all that can be ours

> Come let us put our life in His hands
> Let us seal our choice, having within
> That which is unchanging and eternal
> Let us obey and come in faith believing
> Let us be continually willing

> L O V E - Let Others Value Eternity

19

Sometimes it Seems

Sometimes it seems so hard to do
    That I should bring my all to you
My hopes and plans beyond today
    To cast them off, to go your way

But I know within my troubled soul
    Thy heart in love has planned it so
All things are Thine and Thou dost see
    Thy plan into eternity

And within this shadow Thou hast cast
    A beauty that some day will last
And strength and depth beyond me now
    Within my reach Thou will allow

The past that one can ne'er forget
    With thankfulness will help me yet
To live today and not to fret
    To trust Thee more and more

And if my heart would take its flight
    Thy grace within will hold me tight
To walk by faith and not by sight,
    To love Thee more and more

Leaving

I'm glad it's not left up to me
    To choose by thought or whim
The way that I should go today
    I'm glad it's up to Him

I'm glad my Savior bids me come
    Though sorrow cross my way
For by myself I'd quickly choose
    Another path that day

I'm glad for each experience
    With love He's led me through
The heights my heart could not enjoy
    Before the depths I knew

The hidden treasures He has placed
    Within the path contain
The very things in life I need
    To glorify His name

They are not rocks as I'd implore
    But tools to help me see
The hardness in my heart to all
    That's good and best for me

There are no rocks within the path
    My Savior bids me trod
What lies within fits for the task
    Builds a highway for our God

Joshua 4

So many born in the wilderness
　　　　Kept from the ways of Egypt's land
Nor yet have crossed the Jordan's bank
　　　　Since entered by the faithful band

"What mean ye by these stones?" they say
　　　　As we walk along the pilgrim way
Could they block for us the path ahead
　　　　Obscure our view, hinder instead?

Or are they caused to arrest our step
　　　　To make us pause and reflect a bit
　　　　On the faithful gone before

Within the will of God we find
　　　　A monument be left behind
To tell the story to mankind of victories
　　　　Won by faith: something solid shall remain

And why don't we do some things? they ask
Are they really meant for us today?
Why are they gone from the Path of Life?
Would they surely be a cause to stray?

To keep the goal within our view
And help another's step be true
Deep within the Jordan's main, our past
We leave behind: to bury all things vain

O help the children seek Thy face
To know the power of Thy grace
And help us have the answer Lord
Within our life, the song be heard

That we may know Thy mighty hand
Has on this path caused us to stand
Help our choices of today

Reach

Reach forth to God's hand extended
Grasp the truth found in his son
Be not faithless but believing
Every promise to his own

Forgetting those things behind us
Reach forth to the things ahead
Ever follow Christ's own footsteps
Ever seek his path to tread

One hand reaching tools for building
One hand free to fight the foe
Clasping hands of others near us
Ever reaching for the goal

Forms a building framed together
With no schism, gap or breach
As appointed by God's measure
Each board joins and reaches each

Digging wells and building altars
Ever praying journey on
Every effort God rewards us
Grace sufficient through his son

Humble, contrite hearts now yielded
Prayers of thankfulness and praise
Reflect the life that Jesus gives us
Reach the heart of God who gave

Reaching forth we climb the mountains
Reaching as we meet the sea
Reaching valleys or the deserts
Thus our lot in life will be

But in sacrifice and service
As the years continue on
Extend, maintain the effort
Of the generations gone

Keep on threshing till the vintage
Let vintage reach until we sow
Looking always to the harvest
Continue faithful as you go

Heirs together by his mercy
Reaching every child of God
Extending borders of a family
Knit together by his love

By This Shall All Men Know

By this shall all men know that ye are my disciples
If ye have love one to another

I thought to be an oyster, all cloistered from within
And round I'd grow perfection, each battle now to win
But life is not that way, I've found to my distress
We need the Christ within us, to know our life's been blessed
To break down walls surrounding, the hardness in our heart
Letting his work within us, through others do its part

I thought in prayer and study, to reach the heights sublime
My spirit rose within me, but failed to walk divine
Offense would rise at times, to lift its head and chime
"The humble way of Jesus, his life will not be mine!"
But love-filled lives had touched me, caused my heart to yearn
To find that love within me, I'd claimed in mind to learn

It was God's work accomplished, spirit guided I observed
Through saints and servants yielding, within the place they served
It was Christ's life within them, a candle lit, divine
That brightened each frail vessel and caused their lives to shine
Enduring through the cutting, each diamond facet bright
The dust of which He gathered, to refine and mark my life

We give to God a freedom, which steps of faith have won
To mold us in the likeness, of His beloved son
By faith I now die daily, to walk the path he trod
By faith I see before me, his powerful staff and rod
And though I long to love, to give as given to me
God showed His love through others and taught me to receive

Deut 8:3 *And he humbled thee and suffered thee to hunger, and fed thee with manna, which thou knewest not, neither did thy fathers know: that he might make thee to know that man doth not live by bread alone but by every word that proceedeth out of the mouth of the Lord doth man live.*

Manna
(Exodus 16)

What is this that has gently dropped around my fainting soul
Gentle words that stir the heart and refresh and make me whole

That offers promises of hope, to cheer and comfort me
So close at hand, yet I must stoop to gather what I see

Many a time I've been deceived by illusions in my life
Promising satisfaction, empty words that nurture strife

Will this also, like a dream, leave me hungry in the night
Or will it bear the precious fruit I seek within my life

It reminds me of my thirst within, the empty feeling there
And the many ways I've sought to quench those feelings of despair

It speaks of opportunity in proportion to my need
If I'll take the time and effort to make bread from precious seed

It will strengthen and sustain me, if my heart is what I feed
And reveal the help of heaven, show that God will surely lead

This blessing can be mine today, something safe that I could share
In obeying all these gentle words and the spirit that they bear

Or it could vanish as it came, consumed by life's vain cares
Spoiling any hope of usefulness, revealing the void that's there

Oh to see with clearer vision, our portion every day
Our time of opportunity, ere it vanishes away

To show we've fed on righteousness, true manna from afar
Because all the todays of our life, become just what we are

Our Lamb

If Mary has the same lamb
That all God's children know
Then Mary follows just like us
The path this lamb would go

The path that brings a rest of heart
That gains the higher ground
The path that leads to heaven and home
Where joy and peace are found

For God has only one lamb
His life was given for all
But only those who follow him
Will know his way and call

I was asked to write a poem to go with
Mary had a Little Lamb

Is. 45:11 *Thus saith the LORD, the Holy One of Israel and his Maker: Ask me of things to come concerning my sons and concerning the work of my hands...*

Results!

(Mt.22:29)
You *err in asking*, Jesus said
    Not knowing scripture or God's power
        (Jn.4:10)
You would have asked, had you just known
    God's living gift in his dear son
        (Jn 15:7)
You shall ask and you shall receive
    Abide in him, his words believe
        (Jn 16: 7-13)
The Comforter will guide you then
    Revealing Truth, revealing sin

'Shall not the judge of all the earth
    do right' in all his plan and work

When every seeking soul is led
    To hear the words that Jesus said

And see his life lived out today
    In those who humbly seek to pray:

Lord *may your work in me be done*
    To mold and make me like thy son

* * * *

Ask the right one
Jas. 1:15 *If any lack wisdom, let him ask of God*
Ask the right thing
Jn. 15:7 *If ye abide in me and my words abide in you,*
    Ye shall ask what ye will and it shall be done unto you
Ask the right way
Js. 1:6   *Ask in faith, nothing wavering*
Jn 16:23 *Ask the father in Jesus name*

Overflow

Even the dog partakes of the overflow
    Around our table spread
He seems to enjoy the crumbs that drop
    More than times when he is fed
It's not that he wouldn't desire a place
    Denied his lot, you see
He just can't become what he is not
    The same's with you and me

For a father gives to his children
    The things in life that they need
And they often share with another
    The very things that they eat

Each day the shepherd feeds his flock
    In quietness, alone
Provides the strength for the day ahead
    Before they begin to roam
They know that they are in his care
    And won't journey on alone
They'll keep the nature of the sheep
    No matter how far from home

For our Father gives to his children
    The things in life we all need
And it can benefit others
    When of his spirit we feed

For we are not sheep by nature
       There was a time we weren't in the fold
We could not enjoy the table spread
       Nor the 'beast' in us keep controlled
But we were fed by that lamb-like spirit
       From those in the flock, you see
They had more than enough to satisfy them
       And they shared with you and me

For our Father gives to His children
       The things in life we all need
And it can benefit others
       When of His spirit we feed

That spirit so kind and gentle
       Drew us with bands of love
It showed the abundance of heaven
       That can nourish our souls from above
And the hope of true satisfaction
       Filled us with deep desire
To find ourselves in his presence
       That we too might learn to acquire

All the Father gives to his children
       As lambs brought into the fold
As we're counted as one of the shepherd's
       In exchange for our natures of old

Isaac's Song
(Gen 24:67 - Gen 27)

When the Spirit abides in a body
The two can be influenced as one
Yet the union gives fruit from two sources
Like life that produces two sons

Chorus:
> The struggles in life bring choices
> But there's provision each day for our need
> If we embrace the gospel of Jesus
> God will give us the victory

Before fruit can be borne there's a struggle
But it need not be all in vain
If we heed the message God gives us
And allow the Spirit free reign

For it's human to love life's successes
No matter what field they're found in
But God's spirit will dwell with the lowly
And care for the life that's within

There will be times when our flesh would fail us
But God's spirit always sustains
It has bread and to spare in our weakness
But with it come choices again

It takes effort to sow and be faithful
And labor to uncover a well
It's a struggle to find where God wants us
And then choose to be settled there

But God sees when we dig in the valley
And we dig when all seems in vain
He rewards all our efforts with blessings
Like the faithful of old have obtained

And we'll know the true meaning of blessing
When our 'flesh' is tried as of old
And the Spirit takes heed to the warning
By keeping 'it' under control

We'll be hearing the voice that is speaking
To make flesh all that's in the soul
We'll show the life that is hid in Jesus
Redeeming and making us whole

Then the choices we've made will bring blessing
God will nourish and keep them for thee
When the Spirit is made our true master
And our flesh its servant shall be

Treasures of the Deep

From the depths of ocean waters
From the depths of earth removed
From the depths of sin repented
Come forth pearls and precious jewels

From the fires of deep surrender
Washed from miry clay and dross
Comes refinement God intended
Transformed lives that bear the cross

Precious things brought forth in victory
Treasured virtues we can keep
Enduring riches from his mercy
Are God's blessings of the deep

Lives now sanctified and holy
Cleansed, redeemed, restored again
Lives reflecting Jesus' glory
Will ascend to be with him

From Whence Comes Strength

Strength from heart and purpose, strength from hearth and home

Strength from pure devotion, strength from God alone

Strength from sheer exertion, strength from mind and will

Strength from comrades near us, strength from friendships still

Strength from the banner lifted, strength from the battle cry

Strength from a new day's dawning, or hearing *Taps* in the dusky sky

Strength when duty calls us, strength from rest and food

Strength from relaxation where humor does some good

Strength from pressing forward, strength from hopes renewed

Strength from a past forgiven and from vows we keep in view

Strength from resignation, strength from those we love

Strength from being in their thoughts and the prayers they lift above

Strength from all who live before us, strength from lives within the past

Strength from one who walks beside us, till the journeys done at last

Strength from learning self denial and from convictions that we hold

Strength from where the eagles gather, strength from sheep within the fold

Strength from wisdom, faith and courage, strength from failure and defeat

Strength from looking past the sunset, where eternal shores we meet

Strength from every step we've taken, strength from doing what we can

Strength from keeping true to others, strength from keeping in God's hand

Discipleship

Instruction, counsel and reproof
Are some of life's great learning tools
  To guide us on our way
God's precepts, plumb line, cornerstone
Were all fulfilled in his own son
  Our teacher still today
And Christ as master, shepherd, friend
Reveals his way and truth defends
  The life he lived and gave
With skill he gently leads his sheep
Through winter storms and summer heat
  They're safe within his keep
Pruning and plowing must be done
The sheep are sheared as harvest comes
  In each task there is gain

According to our faith we stand
And faith fulfills what Christ commands
  His righteousness prevails
With truth and mercy side by side
No strength or way is compromised
  Iniquity's removed
Many fall trying to appease
The thief that speaketh with his feet
  They do not use the door
Forgiveness frees the heart of man
And keeps the work in God's own hand
  Revealing honest hearts
And true repentance is 4 things
Each need supplied by what grace brings
  In peace we are restored
    ***

* 4 parts of repentance: I have sinned,
I am sorry, I will change, I will recompense
** reproof (reprove) = to bring to light

Reapers

Someone brought ripe fruit today
And with enthusiastic smile
Canned it before my very eyes

Efficiency was quite condensed
Intense efforts, without mess
And before I had the supper on

Ripened fruit was preserved in jars
And glad rejoicing marked each seal
As the laborer ate his meal

He had not labored o'er the vine
But came upon the fruit in time
And to this work he lent his hand
To see it safely gathered in

Vessels borrowed not a few
Time not lost in vain review
Reaping while the harvest lasts
Secured from winter's stormy blast

And passing on from home to home
A gift of loving kindness went
Adding to each household's store
Summer's riches to enjoy

So we turn in thankfulness
Seeing how some lives are spent
Daily looking o'er the fields
Searching, seeking fruit to seal

Redeeming now while it is day
All that's found along the way
Sharing what's been gathered in
Faithful to the husbandman

There is nothing more reassuring than evidence of confirmation. It settles us and brings a peace and confidence that helps us focus on our next step.

Is There Dew On The Fleece?

Is there dew on the fleece or on the ground
It's surely there if you look around

The evident token of God's great love
That He's heard our cry and sent help from above

If we humble our self and just look around
It's not hard to be where the dew can be found

And if it's God's will that we truly seek
We will not faint, even though we are weak

But loath any thought that would rise from within
That destroys our purpose before we begin

We will not stand where we are sure to fall
We'll recognize the handwriting on the wall

And flee to the place God's strength will abound
And look for the dew that's sure to be found

Look Up!

How strange it seems and wonderful
    That in the darkest night
We see the stars in heaven
    Which aren't visible in the light

For when the sun is shining
    Most brightly all around
Our vision's filled with all the things
    On earth that can be found

We actually see much further
    In the night than in the day
The stars are farther than our sun
    Being lights in their own way

And sometimes our situation
    May seem dark on every side
But it can help us look beyond
    The things of daily life

There is the possibility
    Of looking up while in the night
To see there is a lighted path
    Not hidden from our sight

We may find that in the nighttime
    God will help us to discern
The things in life that matter most
    When life's short race is run

The Greatest Gifts

Sometimes we wonder what we can give
To someone we hold very dear

Life holds out many enticing things
Teasing, yet lost through the years

Promises fading or seen at their cost
Like bubbles bursting in air

Casting their shadows on dreams that are lost
No gift but time can repair

But faith, hope and joy never grow old
And love that is true never dims

They are strength to our soul and balm
To our wounds; the gifts we all need within

And only the giver will know the true cost
And know where the source of it came

For only the giver can show by their life
The gifts of God's son through his name

Within

Oh to be without a Saviour
  Wells without water
  Lamps without oil
  Ships without rudders
  Seeds without soil

Oh how barren, fruitless, useless
All our efforts without Thee
  Salt without savor
  Trees without fruit
  Faith without works
  Judgment without Truth

Lord within my heart doth dwell
  Faith without wavering
  Found without blame
  Lamb without blemish
  World without end

Follow After Charity

I find myself so limited in understanding love
Its qualities encompass truths encouraged from above

Its heights and depths and fullness seem to pass beyond all bounds
And yet we know within Christ's life complete expression is found

It's not life's infatuations that manifest this love
Nor can the truth of it be found in lists "I love because..."

I ponder then the thought embraced "Herein is love", saith he
"Not that we love God, but that he loved us and sent his son to be..."

To think then of the virtues found in love's maturity
The reality of lack within then causes me to plea

That God would teach me how to love as He has first loved me
And put within this life of mine the fruit of Charity

Now Charity begins at home midst kith and kin you see
Begins when little things would fray our generosity

It's not the distant foes we make or passing slights in life
But brothers lacking charity that feed the unchecked strife

When unkind words beget the like and thoughtless deeds give wing
To hurts that compound through the years when started with a sting

These will show how frail we are in loving one another
Show our pride and love of self which does not like to suffer

To think then of the virtues found in love's maturity
The reality of lack within then causes me to plea

That God would teach me how to love as He has first loved me
And put within this life of mine the fruit of Charity

Charity will suffer long, the unjust hurts not measure
Be not provoked when things go wrong, but in God's love find treasure

We would not behave unseemly with Charity in our midst
Nor could we temper deeds or words if not with kindness mixed

It bears all things, believes all things, rejoices in what's right
It faileth not to endure with hope e'en the darkest night

To think then of the virtues found in love's maturity
The reality of lack within then causes me to plea

That God would teach me how to love as He has first loved me
And put within this life of mine the fruit of Charity

Jer. 4:19 *I cannot hold my peace, because thou hast heard, O my soul, the sound of the trumpet and the alarm of war*

Gen. 14:13, 14 *And there came one that had escaped, and told Abram the Hebrew....*
And when Abram heard that his brother was taken captive, he armed his trained servants born in his own house, and pursued them unto Dan...

Ecc. 3:3, 8 *To everything there is a season and a time for every purpose under heaven...*

A time to kill and a time to heal
A time to break and a time to build up
A time to love and a time to hate
A time of war and a time of peace

To Those Who Fight the Battles of the Lord

Oh called to war ye mighty men, valiant, true and brave
To bear the buckler and the sword, chosen by Him who saves
Are ye not helped in the darkest night, though the enemy be near
By the one who leads and hears thy cry, in Him ye need not fear

*

There's nothing like a war to keep one's purpose true and clear
To keep our vision set ahead on things we hold so dear
It causes one to fight for life, for loved ones far and near
To fight for liberty and peace when the bondage we can't bear

**

The cry for peace rings loud and strong

But at the threat of loss

We count the cost

The spoil's the victor's song

***

No one appreciates peace like a soldier
No one loves hearth and home more than he
No one counts life so precious
As the one who does battle for thee

I've enjoyed reading the account of Elisha's ministry found in II Kings. It's one miracle after another. He wasn't afraid of any situation because he had God's Spirit ruling in his life. He had what it took to help others.

Do not fear to follow Jesus, He will lead you safely through

The Borrowed Axe Head

Is the place God dwells too strait for thee
Are you feeling confined instead of free
You're not forced to stay if you cannot see
The abundant provision He has for thee

But to leave and build something different than planned
Is trifling with mercy that's near at hand
And to try to build in another way
Leaves us lacking the tools we'd used yesterday

Then to borrow from men the things they have made
To build the places they dwell in today
Brings sorrow and loss that cannot be retrieved
Because miracles won't happen as when we believed

But if we turn again and cry to the one
Who brings us to Christ as a prodigal son
We see again if we count the cost
It takes something living to reclaim what's been lost

And debtors are we for all that we have
His mercy and grace, His rod and His staff
And the way though narrow it seems to be
Goes on and on through eternity

God's eternal plan centers on the hope of fruitfulness in our lives. To think of God's impartial gifts to all and yet the possibility of never prospering because we fail to take advantage of all the help available.

The Wayside Soil
Matthew 13

I've known the blessing of the rain
Of sun and shadow too
I've been within the sower's reach
As he scattered seeds anew
The open gate was by my path
The plow and rake drew nigh
But I've never had a blade to reap
Though the reapers did pass by
All through the many seasons
This soil of mine lays bare
I've stayed within the sower's reach
Yet outside his bounds of care

Fig Tree
Luke 13

I was planted in a vineyard
    On a very fruitful hill
And my master watches o'er me
    Yet I am unyielding still
I have never changed three seasons
    Though the dresser grooms the vines
I'm untouched by all his efforts
    Though he's very close at times
But I'm understanding mercy
    I'm now willing for his care
Now I know his depth of goodness
    Since he sought my life to spare

The Precious Seed
Psalm 126

The tiller plowed the hardened soil
    The sower shed his tears
And again I take the lowly place
    Their investment through the years
The labor of the husbandman
    Prepares for miracles to come
But God supplies my greater needs
    Of life and rain and sun
Anchored and growing still
    Willing for the process of time
I am the upright sheaf of wheat
    I am the fruitful vine

Gen. 37:3 *Now Israel loved Joseph more than all his children, because he was the son of his old age; and he made him a coat of many colors.*

Gen. 44:20 *We have a father, an old man, and a child of his old age, a little one . . . and his father loveth him.*

A lot of the "tests" that Joseph inflicted on his brothers had to do with how they treated the youngest among them. It is sobering to consider what stirs in our heart when we see the blessings and rewards of the one who takes the lowest (least) place. It's wonderful to see that Joseph's brothers learned to value and care for the things their father loved. They learned to rejoice when the little child was honored above them. They learned to protect him and esteem him more precious than their own lives.

Unto us a child is born
(Is. 9:6)

A coat of many colors, proclaimed his father's love
An honored place that bypassed rank, and by favor rose above

> It rankled them at every turn
> While their ill report caused no concern
> But fueled resentment and envy more
> Until their thoughts only hatred bore

"I seek my brethren: tell me I pray thee, where they feed"

> His brothers stripped him of his coat
> And robbed him of his home
> But couldn't take from him the love
> That he had always known

> The love to do his father's will
> To be true to what was shown
> Of future days of glory
> Though by experience, yet unknown

Could we know the subtle testing of our spirit through each day
We'd be conscious of our thoughts, for our feet may pass that way
And time will bring full circle, our deeds, we'll one day learn
Have consequence still waiting, the truth we've yet to discern

> And one day every knee did bow
> In honor to this one
> Who'd been the least in all his house
> And yet the favored son

> And he sought to see their willingness
> To love what his father loved
> To see their care for the least in their midst
> And rejoice that it's blessed from above

And they saw their brother as he was: his fame and majesty
And knew remorse for the part they had played
In his pain and agony

> Yet God had sent him on ahead
> To preserve their posterity
> To bring them to a place of rest
> Where he could nourish and feed

"I seek my brethren: tell me I pray thee, where they feed"

51

Moses

The son of Pharaoh's daughter, a privileged boy was he

Learned in Egyptian's wisdom, mighty in word and deed

And yet another's son was he, nourished in captivity

A son of Levi still to be, to claim an eternal home

> Could we compare the contrast here
>> And see things as they will appear
> And when we contemplate the cost
>> Of earthly joys that might be lost
>> In gaining Heaven's best

> May we consider those of yore
>> Who endured reproach, forsook far more
> Who saw the treasure yet to be
>> Far greater in eternity
>> And willingly left all

And when we think of Moses, encouraged we can be

His faithful self- denying, spoke from eternity

For even Christ who saw him, was moved to help us see

Dying lives are living proof they got the victory

An Image of Gold
(Daniel)

The image of gold resembled a man
The standard of power and might

Not just an image a deity too
Demanding respect day and night

All honors it claimed for riches and fame
Sweet music to everyone's ears

An image of gold so desired by all
No thought of its cost through the years

This image so rare, dictating their lives
Bringing each one to their knees

And though they arise their fulfillment lies
Bound first to this one they must please

It's a gold standard to worship and praise
A passion that burns without trial

An image man sees that captures to please
Not fearing that Satan beguiles

A mistaken way that vanishes one day
Not worthy to withstand the fire

But, approved of God, no other desire
In hearts both yielded and willing

The image of Christ, worked in a life
Exceeds even all things compelling

53

Circumstance
(Psalm 40, Daniel 2)

The Bible speaks of two who had
> Their feet in miry clay
And by themselves they had no control
> Over how they got that way
It speaks of one whose superior power
> Made him a king of kings
But the future of his might and fame
> Was not within his reigns
He had no control beyond the grave
> Over what he left behind
The vision showed him all that he left
> Was surely to decline
And not only that, but it would count
> As nothing in that day
When the God of heaven set up his throne
> And destroyed everything in its way
This earthly king who dreamed this dream
> Had never known his plight
But the truth about the greater king
> Was put within his sight

He was forewarned in mercy
From coming wrath to flee
When the servant clearly told him
Of all that was to be
To acknowledge that he needed help
Was a humbling choice to make
But we see the results of crying out
When the other man's place we take
From miry clay he was lifted up
And established in the way
His feet were set upon the rock
That preserves us still today
He was saved from all that would destroy
And filled with songs of praise
For the wonderful works of God he knew
His mercy, his love and his grace
And his words of praise still linger
For all who would heed his plea
That the God of Heaven can help us
No matter what our circumstance be

The Eunuch and the Captive
(Daniel 1- Luke 12)

The eunuch stood and pondered a youthful man's request
With wonder and amazement mixed with fear at his behest
How could it be that one free born would not desire a feast
But ask for pulse and water as a child or slave might eat
Not just for him alone he asked this favor to impart
But for others standing close to him, with purpose in each heart

He marveled at their willingness, admired their simplicity
Could defilement really come from what his own king found worthy
To stand approved before his king was all that really mattered
Could it be these men before him feared a greater lord and master
How was it they could prosper and serve with gladness free
Have treasure hid within their lives from a god he couldn't see

The eunuch knew he served a king of power, greed and fame
And lives weren't precious in his sight, nor kindness ere his aim
His conqueror laid up treasure here on earth for all to see
His rule of fear could never bring devotion from men like he
He'd never known of mercy, nor was hope ever his to be
But bound before him now stood one who spoke with liberty

By faith he serves a living God, his comfort in distress
Whose ways are all in peace and truth and full of righteousness
His lord and master cares for him and all that are his own
It shows upon his countenance as a favored gift bestowed
His wisdom, knowledge, grace and skill are from his God above
Who gives to those who ask of him and obey him out of love

He desires that I would prove his word in the days ahead to see
If all he said would come to pass and deal accordingly
So the eunuch watched the captive lads and saw them gain the more
In feeding on the simple things proved them stronger o'er and o'er
He saw them stand before his king in matters great and small
And answer all his questionings, honoring God in all

Ps 116 *Daniel influenced kings and kingdoms as a servant of servants.*
He fed his faith not just his body. He served God not just man and he
paid his vows.

I've enjoyed some parables and parallels in Samson's life that show glimpses of the gospel story and the character of Christ. God hates sin but he loves a perishing world and he puts that same love into the hearts of his sent ones. They are not always perfect vessels, but they are useful vessels.

Judges 15:17 *"and it came to pass when he had made an end of speaking, that he cast away the jawbone out of his hand, and called that place Ramoth-lehi"*

Jawbone -v.t. *to influence by persuasion, especially by public appeal rather than exertion of force or authority*

Samson

They could not understand why he
Would seek to love the enemy
Would speak in kindness and would give
Garments to lives unworthy lived

They could not understand how he
Could always get the victory
Why he would not be bound by all
That caused an ordinary man to fall

And yet we might begin to see
How this friend of sinners came to be
The one who battled not with sword
But preached to all a living word

For we know God put within his hand
The thing that delivers the soul of man
And he could conquer one by one
And smite each heart with just his tongue

And it's not hard to understand
There's fewer enemy in the land
Though foe and friend betrayed alike
God strengthened him to give his life

What Shall Be Thy Rising Up?
(Proverbs 24:16)

What shall be thy rising up
When at the close of day
Thy sins be cast into a heap
That will not flee away

But bind thee closer to the ground
From which the clay is formed
What will be thy rising up
Before a new day's born

What will be thy rising up
When travail doth mock thy soul
When hopes are dashed and pride would see
A future uncontrolled

What can help thee rise above
The snares of death that bind
The thoughts and words and actions
Found in all mankind

And what can free the soul of man
When at the close of day
He finds that he has erred again
In walking in God's way

The fall of man, his rising up
Was seen and planned in heaven
A full repentance through God's son
Is the blood bought gift that's given

Study on Jonah

Oh Father wilt thou help me learn to love thy mercy seat

To put my faith and effort still to keep the lambs and sheep

I've fed the lambs and fed the sheep and what could I do more

But once again thou sayest to me, "Just feed them o'er and o'er"

Yet flesh would say "It is too far, they've gone astray this time"

Let come what may, I'll go my way, let them reap their own decline

And tho my heart be hard as stone, my ear shut to thy voice

Thou still prepares a way for me to see the better choice

For turning from the vows I've made, the storms of life rage on

Yet without thee, this time I fear, the hurts and damage done

Then from the depths my prayer came forth

To retrieve one such as me

Who was cast out into the deep, with no hope of being free

I will arise and do thy will, I'll pay that that I've vowed

But lacking that same mercy shown was all my heart allowed

Now with thanks to thee I'll lift my voice

With others share my gain and loss

Because once more Thy kindness shown

Had pity on this life I own, to remove again the dross

The California Redwood

Walking along the beaten path that led me up the hill
Admiring all the beauty that progressed to grander still
I paused to absorb the handiwork begun in antiquity
To appreciate in a fuller sense

Its Silent Testimony

Before me stood a massive tree that began as any shoot
But nature's masterpiece took years to reach from tip to root

Its greatness was achieved in living day by day
Not setting limits to its growth, it's growing still today

Still undaunted by the fires, the pestilence, the drought
It fills its place amidst the grove, unheard the voice of doubt

But a reverent quietness surrounds me as I gaze
This upright pillar of today was produced by upright yesterdays

And no words needed to be spoken
It was all God had intended it to be

Let Him now create unhindered, till His noble work is done

Hast Thou Considered My Servant Job?

There was a man whom Satan tried to prove his faith was vain
And in a moment's time he took every treasure Job had gained
The substance he had labored for, the children he had blessed
His health and strength and joy in life; the hope he had possessed

Not just the efforts of his prayers, the fruit was now gone too
And thus erased his heart now heard the thoughts of those he knew
To grief was added torment, as one by one expressed
Their doubts in God's true faithfulness and Job's own uprightness

There came a time Job cursed the day that he was ever born
And days when all his fears were brought to light and scorned
But in all this he never sinned nor charged God foolishly
His soul was saved from harm by what Job did continually

He rose up early every morning to sacrifice and pray
And fell to worship on the ground in thankfulness always
The sweet communion that he knew; the work which was wrought
Was manifest to others, because he lived what God had taught

He waited in affliction, though crying in despair
Asked God to show and make him know his judgments and his care
His every word and work and way was measured by God's will
And though the former days were gone, he knew God loved him still

Then through the dark confusion, Job heard again God's voice
Giving glorious strength and wisdom, demanding a clearer choice
My servant who is faithful in all he said of me
Will know my blessing even more because he prays for thee

John 4:4 *What had at one time been visible evidence of victory in the lives of God's people had now become just a ritual. There was nothing in their lives that gave meaning to their service.*

Jacob's Well

A place of renown, still remembered today
A memory now marred by confusion and shame

A well dug by forefathers, again and again
Who labored in faith and a blessing obtained

This well sustained life for the thirsty of heart
It stood for the promise God's will would impart

But hindered by bondage, in lives that were vain
This inheritance stood waiting, God's children to claim

Until Jesus Came

The story of Job tells us that he died a very rich man.
Many see only that his natural wealth doubled. But if
we look more closely, we see in his life an increase of
greater substance. This was his greatest blessing from God.

The Double Portion
(Job 42:12)

The hedge that once seemed broken down
    On every side of life
When disappointments, sorrow, loss
    Brought tears and earthly strife
Now appears to all renewed
    And blessed by God the more
What God allowed within a life
    He could heal and then restore

God repaired a broken home
    A broken marriage vow
And friendships marred by broken trusts
    Were mended too somehow
All that was his earthly gain
    Was doubled from before
But while passing through the valley
    His spirit gained the more

For from the tears and ashes a greater repentance came
And as his understanding grew, his speech was not the same
The revelation he received of God's presence everywhere
Gave him wonderful assurance and more effectual prayer

A humble man he now was known in latter life to be
And a greater family was now his company
The riches shared by one and all were now his portion too
And what he gave to others was what he'd gained in truth

65

A Life That Speaks
(Isaiah 61)

I will give thanks for years now spent
    To know my time on earth was lent
To have known the One from heaven sent
    To save my life for aye

I will not fear tomorrow
    I have learned through tears and sorrow
That my strength and joy are in Thy hand
    With mine in thine alone

I do not fear the grave
    He may take me ere the morning light
I've crossed the valleys, born the gale
    The sun has risen without fail
        And my Lord was by my side

I do rejoice with the reaper's song
    I've seen the results of seed that was sown
With beauty for ashes He's faithful to give
    And the oil of joy for our mourning

The anointing of God brings treasure full store
    In exchange for life's earthly riches
And the song that is sung when our liberties won
    Lifts the cloud with a garment of praises

Remembering
(II Kings 2:10)

The life of a servant of God
    Was taken from view today
His mantle no longer will hide
    All God's work concerning the clay

Can we see what carried him onward
    Marked each choice every step of the way
Will we find death cannot rob the soul
    Of the faithful who serve God always

Will it prompt greater depth to our cry
    And willingness because of our need
Will we desire more courage and strength
    To be examples in word and in deed

For it's not the plowing that's hard
    Nor the labor in gathering sheaves
But hard it is often to bow
    And continue in faith to believe

God seeks for those willing to journey
    Upholding his life and his way
He'll strengthen their vision and purpose
    Renewing his spirit each day

Mantling each one in his service
    Saying peace rule and reign in each heart
Holding high the life lived before us
    Enfolding lights with love from afar

67

Joab
(I Kings 1)

A trumpet sounding above the noise
Its purpose ringing clear
Had shot alarm through a mighty man
And filled his heart with fear

Who gave command that this be done
Was the captain's silent cry
But the message from the throne itself
Could not his thoughts belie

How came he here to be amongst the crowd
That now was scorned
Not standing with the King of Kings
Whose allegiance he had sworn

How came his hand to help exalt
The one not chosen heir
Could he save him now from all the woe
That he had brought to bear

How called he some to come and dine
And refused those now at hand
Who filled their rightful place amongst
The chosen of the land

How was it he, who led the host
Had gone so far astray
When the kingdom's crown was placed upon
Another's brow that day

Yet glancing o'er the goodly crowd
He failed to see the thing
Had lacked from the beginning
David's prophet, priest and king!

Alaska

Through the mist of the morning
    Mountains reached for the sky
Simple nature abounded
    No restrictions applied

Unspoiled and unspotted
    Boundless treasures, its own
Yet there's much contradiction
    In this fierceness so bold

How fragile its nature
    Untempered its foes
Its vast open spaces
    Touched by God's hand alone

How subtle the forces
    Shaping all that we see
How fair were its users
    Taking only their need

Untold were its prospects
    Though countless ages passed by
Asleep to the future
    Never dreamed it would die

But I ponder the virtue
    Of just living alone
Though noble to think that
    We've not harmed anyone

There's a purpose and season
    To all God has made
It shapes all our future
    Returns all that we've saved

And it offers the promise
    We can grasp every day
To follow a pathway
    That will never decay

Home Again

50 years have come and gone
And the tables now have turned

From one home of many years
Across the waters, memories dear

With companions by my side
Shifting for ourselves, oft-times

Now to spend more time alone
Moving oft from home to home

Packing to unpack again
This the 100 fold I gain

Many homes and many faces
All my routine now embraces

Not a list or book or text
Guides to where or what is next

Seeing things I took for granted
Removed, returned, by others handed

But looking back, as I recall
Those very things aren't changed at all

For when I was a lad at home
Others did what I could have done

And home again, I now can see
How it was done so willingly

And I can do what *they will do*
For they can't do what I have done

Matthew 27 / Philippians 3:10

Lord help us find in the final hours
    The help that was given to Thee
When those who knew us best are gone
    And alone we may seem to be
Help us fight the good fight of faith
    So others looking on may see
Our hope and joy and confidence
    That still abounds in Thee

Help all our words and thoughts and deeds
    Proclaim our faith and love
That others who may know Thee not
    Might look to Thee above
And Father, though our strength seems frail
    As keener grows the fight
Increase those things which Thou hast wrought
    To bring victory by Thy might

Let more by grace our lives control
    Let more Thy Spirit feed
Let more our willingness to yield
    Yet more and more to Thee
Till by Thy grace we come at last
    To face the final hour
"Strong in the strength which He supplies"
    Our only hope and power

And Jesus I would thank Thee more
    For helping me to see
That Thou alone in death didst face
    The cry that was meant for me
That while I yet have life within
    I might face eternity
With full assurance every hour
    I will not forsaken be

She Who Tends the Garden
(*That nourishes the heart*)

Oft times we don't appreciate
    The beauty or the space

That surrounds our lives
    Through loving hands

Offering a place to meditate

We're so busy rushing here and there
    With no time to sit or see

This atmosphere of quiet rest
    Though it beckons you and me

Its order blends with nature's ways
    We're engulfed in serenity

As even a passing glance that's cast
    Delights in what it sees

Each vantage point shows a tapestry
    Of color, light and skill

And expresses a passion and a love
    And a vital need that's there

There is a Place of Quiet Rest
Near to the heart of God

As I leaned upon a railing, looking at the falls
Engrossed in all the turbulence, the tumult and the noise
I'm not aware how long it took before my eyes were drawn
To see a sight more marvelous than the falls I looked upon

For down below the surface, along the slippery slopes
Clung numerous, delicate fallen leaves shimmering in the dusk
They did not move from mossy rock swept by the rushing stream
But quietly, content they lay; a picture calm, serene

I wondered what their anchor was, what was the greater force
That held them bound unto the rock, unmoved by any source
For had they settled quietly in pools along the shore
I never would have taken note or thought upon it more

But now the contrast stirred my heart to make impressions there
To see the place of safety lay beneath the cause of care
To look beyond the things we see or what we think we know
And find the place of full release below the currents flow

Will draw us to a place of rest where all our cries are known
A place upon the rock where we must cling to God alone
That place is deeper than our fears and deeper than our woe
But it's nearer to the heart of God, where living waters flow

Sunday Morning

A singular experience happened recently
A calm, a feeling of release was felt so intently
It caused me to awake from sleep
As I became aware of a quiet peace
Within my soul, replacing struggles there

It was almost like a picture, the words that spoke
You see. Giving answer to the why within, that
Had been plaguing me. Time was a fluid moment
Succeeded by a voice, acknowledging the victory was
In part, some other's choice

"Someone has prayed for me by name" This voice
Within me said. And I, conscious of the import
Answered in its stead, "Oh thank you, though I know
Not who spent time so earnestly. Your fervent, constant,
Instant prayer has much availed for me"

Then with those thoughts I must confess what I
Considered next: How often the names I pray for too
I lump with all the rest. How often I cut short my prayers
Because of some excuse. How many a battle
Could have been won by defeating Satan's ruse

I'd Never Been To Mandan
(Convention grounds)

I'd never been to Mandan, but I knew just what I'd find
There would be lots of friendly faces, of the familiar kind

The meeting and the dining tent would have the needful stuff
The place for moms and tots to stay was filled with just enough

There'd be bunks galore for younger folks and cots for older ones
And hookups for the motor homes, a place for everyone

And having all these needs met, there would abound much more
For every soul a quiet place to quicken and restore

A place to feed the hungry heart and cast away doubt and fear
To share our thankfulness with all and sing some songs of cheer

And among the crowd of friendly folks some special ones would be
Those who'd helped me in my early days the truth of God to see

And names that I had only heard, were there in person too
And some I had not met before, before I left, I knew

I got to show my folks around and I really didn't mind
I'd never been to Mandan but I knew just what I'd find

And if I'm asked, "What's heaven like?" Would I only smile and guess
I've never been to heaven but I know that it's God's best

The joy and help we've all known here, will there much more abound
And I will share my thankfulness for a taste of all that's found

75

Hebrews 9

He's dead! They cried
His body lies within the tomb!

And what remains for us
Except a spirit filled with doom!

But Wait! They say
Was there not left one last request?

One granted wish
For those who mourn his passing?

His last behest!
What left he as an inheritance?

His life is gone. They sighed
What can he now give of benefit to others?

I scarce can comprehend
"The Holiest is open now and we may enter in"

And now before the throne of grace
My savior pleads on my behalf

And grace and mercy now extends
To all who find this open path!

What is it?
(Hebrews 10:19-22)

On the table wine and bread, covered by a cloth
Until the time I partake of it, its form is all but lost

But I take by faith what men rarely see
Christ's life has opened the way for me

To enter God's presence and see what Christ saw
For he opened for me the Holiest of all

Now I can see clearly the Life and the Way
The provision that helps me to serve day by day

I see all God's promises found in his Word
I see His provisions and service preferred

I see what will help me to win in the race
For Christ's body and blood promise mercy and grace

His life accepted, his death on the tree
The remembrance of both are coming to me

In prayers of thankfulness and hymns of praise
My life and my vows I rededicate

To love and to live the new life I gained
When Christ through his life rent the veil in twain

Fellowship

One in heart, in mind and spirit

We may not see the tears and hands that
>Burnish breastplate, shield or sword

We may not hear the prayers when others
>Parted lips to God implore

But we may see when others lend a hand, or
>Watch upon the ramparts through the land

And we may hear when weary in the fight
>A song that claims the victory is in sight

And gaining liberty of spirit, mind and soul
>We know the unity of a common goal

Candles

There was a time, now years ago, I still recall today
The time I set my heart to seek God's perfect truth and way

I did not trust my own attempts to guide my feet aright
Nor could I see a path ahead without a little light

The various ways one tries to find the peace we all would know
I now did ask on bended knee, and sought what God would show

    And while I waited anxiously, I watched with curiosity
    Two young girls that were set by me

I saw them through my window, the many times they passed
And I noticed something different and it prompted me to ask

Why their youthful convictions had impacted me so
And where they went to church, because I thought I'd like to go

Their response was simple and sincere and wrapped with honesty
They sought to follow Jesus, the way it was meant to be

And though I've read it many times, it's still a mystery
How God can use obedience to be our light to see

The word 'good' is used almost 1000 times in the Bible. Webster's defines good as a 'term of approval meaning *as it should be*; suitable and beneficial to a purpose.'

The Bible is often referred to as 'the good book.' The beginning of Genesis recounts the goodness of God's word spoken and accomplished in the manner he intended.

King Solomon by wisdom sought to find out all that was good and worthwhile in life. The book of Ecclesiastes weighs the benefits of all man's labors and concludes that life is temporary and our enjoyments are a fleeting reward with zero purpose or meaning unless we consider God and his eternal plan. His advice to all is to fear God and keep his commandments. This should occupy our thoughts and time now because there is a judgment and eternity to come.

Jeremiah 6:16 - *seek and ask for the old paths where is the good way*
I Kings 3:9 - *discern between good and bad*
Isaiah 7:15 - *know to refuse the evil and choose the good*
Romans 12:18 - *in my flesh dwells no good thing: for to will is present with me*
Philippians 1:6 - *he which hath begun a good work in you will perform it*
Ephesians 2:10-*we are his workmanship, created in Christ Jesus unto good works*
III John 11-*he that doeth good is of God: but he that doeth evil hath not seen God.*

Who Will Show us any Good?

There be many that say
Who will shew us any good?
Psalm 4:6

Who will stand against the foe
Armed with what God's children know

Who will show when all is night
God still reveals to us his light

Who will show the goal ahead
Is beyond the dictates man has said

Who will simply watch and pray
And be what God has willed today

Who, in silence, will bring forth
A quiet spirits gentle voice

Who will speak a word in season
Truth that overcomes man's reason

Who will show that victory brings
The overcoming of lesser things

Who can warn when it's today
By simply walking in God's way

There is none that doeth good
But Christ within works 'as it should'

Others see our choices made
Mark a path that Jesus laid

Showing that we understand, the good
Of what God's heart has planned

Exposing things misunderstood
A light revealing God is good

81

Standing Firm

I watched the wind through the trees today
      They bowed and bent in a stately sway
Until the gusts became a roar
      And leaves and branches flew the more

The trees spoke loudly in the gale
      But it was the wind that I heard wail
They seemed with one accord to say
      "Stand firm and bend some more today"

I saw the clouds all scurry by
      As wind and weather touched the sky
But steadfast, firm, within the fray
      Were trees that stood their ground today

And though the winds are fierce and strong
      Much seed is scattered in the storm
And when the calm replaced the rage
      Both flowers and buds remained unchanged

I learned some lessons from the trees
      When winds of time and change will blow
Just calmly bend, let some things go
      And keep grounded in the things I know

Part II
Growing Panes
Poems of Family, Faith, and Friends

*There are many windows of opportunity to learn
the lessons of life among those who have loved us
and we have loved in return.*

Yesterday

It's gone!

I can not catch it

So removed from time and place

The years have since erased it

Though I look

The sights can not reclaim

The memories reborn by other senses

I now taste and hear and smell

The things I cannot see

It's all that's left, except reverie

Going Home

I dropped a box today and
Out spilled letters from bygone days
Things that I have saved
Important to me in many ways

Yet with uncertain future
To Whom It May Concern
When my short journey here is done
And I go home

A picture with no name
Once a treasure she did claim
Yet bequeathed to me
For she was going home

What am I to do with these? She said
And with hand held out to me
She gave it
For they long since were home

Her Bible she kept near
A source of comfort still
While she was looking there
Not here

Profiles in Black and White

Aged with time and varying care
Unframed, unnamed and silent stare
The face and form of family past
Preserved in a precarious way to last
    The passing of the years

I knew them not except to be
A distant relative to me
And though their lives might fill a book
They yielded not to inquiring look
    But solemn, grim remained

Had I means to make a prism of those shades of black and white
I would open up the spectrum of the tales within each life

Colorful, I'm sure they'd be with every shade and hue
As each unfolded story led to remembrances anew

And though years have separated us and times have changed it's true
A common thread might bind us to a past we never knew

We might see the same experience in just a different way
Know the pioneering spirit as in those of yesterday

Within each one we all would see the courage just to live
To pass uncharted pathways that our lot in life would give

To mix the hard work with some fun and face life's good or ills
To give our best to what is best and do without the frills

We'd know that faith is needed, to convictions we'd hold true
We'd lend a hand to others, keep on helping till it's through

We'd spend some time to reflect a bit on why God put us here
To see the path that continues on when death would draw us near

I wondered too what they might see while staring out at me
Would I measure up to all the good that's in the family tree

Leaving Marks

A branding and a barbecue
With lots of sun and smiles
An afternoon to stop and share
In family things worthwhile

Five benches strewn around the yard
And branding irons a smoking
The hurry and the bustle
Not complete without some joking

The cousins came from miles around
(Some more distant than the others)
To reunite the feeling of
A kinship sparked in brothers

Memories of the by-gone years
Were talked about a lot
And we celebrated present joys
As each would add a jot

Each finished bench is quite a sight
As 40 brands now claim
To be identified with all the marks
That bear the ELKIN name

And it's prompted me to consider more
The marks obtained by others
To want to share in all that makes
Us sisters and as brothers

At Season's End

Underneath the sunlit sky
    I watched as bitter cold swept by
The grass and trees all empty now
    Had cast their shadows and somehow
        Ceased to want to play

The prairie stretched for miles around
    The once soft earth was hard I found
The fields that once to plow gave heed
    Now stood in silence, without seed
        Frail relics of the past

All that remains at season's end
    Are memories of what once had been
And though it's bleak, this sight I see
    I'm reminded of eternity
        And all that's without end

They say all nature does His will
    Only to man gives He freedom still
To him, He gives both chance and time
    To fit into His plan divine
        To bear the precious seed

So let that be sown within our heart
    That fits us for the better part
When earth lends neither woe nor charm
    But heaven waits with open arms

Let not it be at season's end
    Just memories of what might have been
But fruit within our lives to see
    We had prepared for eternity

This Shall be a Testimony

Swifter than a weaver's shuttle
Ceased the spark of life
Choices now forever chosen
Amidst the joy and strife

Quietly they came and listened
Reverently they left
Surrounding those who now were mourning
They paid their last respects

Unknown strangers (workers, saints)
Who signed their names, like others
But with their presence gave support
To one who'd lost his brother

If There's a Rest, You Still Have a Part

Sometimes the music stops playing
Sometimes the singing will cease
Sometimes we must pause in our actions
If there's a rest, we must not miss the beat

Don't hasten the moments of living
Nor shrink from the path that's in view
Every step of your journeys been measured
In every part, there is something to do

Were it not for the moments of resting
That keeps the work of others in view
We might not find, the time to re-echo
All our heart would be saying to do

All the words that never were spoken
All the things we might see from afar
Come in moments of peaceful reflection
Like the rests between the notes on a bar

Reflect on time, when the melodies fading
The harmony that's never your part
See the spaces and notes flow together
Even though you stop playing your part

Though the rests may keep on repeating
Measured time marks each moment anew
Hear the sounds of the silence retreating
Know each line holds the melody true

Remember, when the music's still playing
The pause is not meant for regret
Never feel that you've just been forgotten
Because the song is not over yet

See the hand that can soften the discord
That will beckon you on if it can
The one who knows the purpose and reasons
For each rest that was a part of His plan

Weavings

There is a thread within our lives
That passes to and fro
Connecting all the days and years
As experiences come and go

There are many patterns formed
In the tapestry of life
There are various degrees of tension
As we work through fears and strife

The texture, whether rough or smooth,
Adds dimension to our years
The threads are colored by our thoughts
Some are softened by our tears

Our choices and accomplishments
Are woven side by side
And changes in direction
Mark the path the shuttle glides

There may be some unraveled ends
Times we started something new
But they are on the other side
The side we show to few

Where knots and imperfections are
And the pattern's less distinct
But it's the side where change occurs
And we work out all the kinks

It is the side of who we are
For the pattern on display
That when exposed unselfishly
Helps others on their way

94

The Things I Left Behind

If I could, I would have taken the night sky
Seeing the Milky Way instead of the aura of city lights

I would have taken the fragrance of fresh mown hay
And the clover by the driveway

If I could, I would spread again the beautiful flax field
Like a damask cloth of delft blue

I would take the serenity of vast open spaces
The rolling wheat fields

Instead, I took memories of laughter and family
I took a feeling of kinship and a renewed sense of self

I took tokens of accumulated treasures handed down
Through the generations

I took strength for the present and hope for the future
I took pictures of columbine and roses blooming

And the ashes laid to rest on the prairie hill

An Inheritance Unfading

It truly is a miracle
To see those going on
While passing through the fires of life
Remaining true and strong

It truly is the work of God
When in a life we see
A thankful heart that's full of joy
And knows humility

It's wonderful when full of life
Though life's filled days are gone
The things that mattered most in life
Are the ones that carry on

The soft and tender heart that speaks
Of God's great mercies new
The life behind a countenance
We want to keep in view

How wonderful when lives are gone
Their testimonies stay
To remind us of their faith and love
In God's true will and way

How precious are His promises
How sweet the journey through
When knowing fellowship with His son
And those who love Him too

For it's the things that we've embraced
In life that carry on
The temporal things will one day fade
What matters is our song!

Be Ready

I was reading an article on sailing
    Of which I know little about
But I noticed a thought worth repeating
    A warning to all, no doubt

It cautioned about changes in weather
    And changes in currents and tides
But it said with strict adherence
    To be ready ahead of time

To do in advance all that's needed
    Before it needs to be done
Was the theme that was often repeated
    As I continued to read along

So as we speed on our journey
    With choices that confront us today
Be safe, be alert, and be ready
    For the wind may change today

We may be caught in the current
    Or the tide may pull us about
And our life may depend on the things we did
    Before we ever set out

Yes be prepared in the morning
    It will steady our course for the day
And whatever may come without warning
    We will not regret that we prayed

Our Heart's Treasure
(Matthew 6:21)

I used to test myself at times to prove my moderation
To see if all I did possess was not a complication
I would ask myself if all were lost could you leave without dismay
If more important things came up could you simply walk away
And through the years I tried to find a balance in my choice
Some things I kept for beauty's sake but most was useful stuff
Then there came a turning point in all my grand design
An inheritance of no small means filled up this house of mine
And everything that I received had memories attached
Of loved ones from my family some generations past
Some with stories to pass on, some of value to just one
But all were evidence someone had used them with much care
It worries me to some extent that I'm emotionally content
To have this stuff around
It somehow fills the void at times where children filled this life of mine
And family members that I loved were still not far away
And I find I want to introduce each piece I own as evidence
Of lives that now are gone
I know with time this too will change but it's a disconcerting thing
To think that what's now in my care will not become a burden
But still retain some usefulness and be enjoyed with thankfulness
To remind us now that life is short and our memories store treasures
And things are only things

I Did Not Hear It Come

I did not hear it come
But all was brighter
In the moonlight
And cozy warm inside

Enough of sleep
I must take a peek
And see what now adorns
The countryside

All that was stark
And barren
Now aglow
All clothed in snow

I Could Never Fill Your Shoes

If I could see things as you do
    I'd need to walk within your shoes

But it's hard to wear what doesn't fit
    I never would get used to it

But if we walk …along… beside
    And show and share instead of chide

We might enlarge the view we see
    Considering you and considering me

The course we take might meander some
    Not be the short cut used by one

But to understand another's view
    The heart and mind must listen too

For we must show how much we care
    When it's the others turn to share

And I could grow and you could too
    Though we'd never fill each other's shoe

On Your Anniversary

It was a beautiful wedding
　And a beautiful bride!

How many days in between
　And weeks beside

Only two can know
　Twix the ebb and the flow

The love and the trust
　That continued to grow

So in remembering today
　The commitment you made

And all that's been shared
　When that foundation was laid

That strengthened you both
　In good times and not

And was a treasure beheld
　That encouraged a lot

From those far and near
　Sending wishes today

And remembering the joy
　And the love they relay

May you savor the memories
　You've shared side by side

Congratulations to you!
　And a kiss for the bride!

I have often pondered Gen.1:26, 27and Gen.2:7, 18-23
It must be considered from heaven's perspective.
What was needed?
Something was taken out of man and enlarged.

I am He

Personified and magnified
The side he does not wish to see
I was made to be

Though outward form is all we see
The same old clay fills you and me
Yet I, the second one, feel free
To first express my needs

Do not confuse the issue of
Which one deserves the greater love
Bigness and largeness are not the same
And the tasks at hand are on a higher plane

And meant to be a help to reach
And see the worth of gaining each
A Nobler Call

I am She

The Counterbalance

(The encounter)
Introduce to me your counterpart
          Your mate; equivalent
The one you took in marriage vows
          To be your compliment
The one whose destiny you chose
          To make your life complete
Introduce me to your counterpart
          Your equilibrium, so to speak

(To counter)
What? (*You say*) It cannot be
          They are so completely opposite me
How can it be that I did choose
          Someone who counters my every move
In every way we do oppose
          It's no support, we come to blows
A counterpart I cannot see
          In one who constantly frustrates me

(The re-counter)
I wanted one to lean upon
          Where I was weak, they would be strong
I wanted my way, not compromise
          I wanted my visions realized
I wanted agreement and unity
          I wanted admiration, not scrutiny
The only equality I can see
          Is a total lack of sympathy

104

(To counterpoise)
But by degrees as time goes on
      There's a shifting in who's right or wrong
New strategies, techniques are used
      Affecting actions, mellowing moods
Influencing higher attitudes
      Countering careless, selfish words
Until one day, you both can see
      We've been there, done that, don't repeat

(The counterpart)
There comes a time, through thick and thin
      They are your equilibrium
Their life and yours are intertwined
      By all you've gained or left behind
The compliment of each is seen
      By all you to each other mean
A force to balance every weight
      A counterpart that is complete

* * *

Counterpoise - to bring into equilibrium by an equal
   opposing power or force, to furnish an equivalent
Counterbalance - A weight balancing another weight
Counterpart - A person closely resembling another in function,
   One of two parts that fit, complete or compliment one another
To Counter - in opposition, contrary, to deliver counter action,
   designed to thwart, frustrate, off set, parry (in response to)

After 25 Years

Somehow we thought our chosen one
    Would be our mirror image
It was quite a shock to find them not
    Connected to our lineage

But when united as we were
    With much that brought us blessing
We were often two in everything
    Which was surprising and distressing

Two minds and wills and emotions
    Wreck havoc with our vows
To be one in heart and purpose
    Was a challenge we learned to allow

For time and experience taught us
    The "other half" makes up our whole
We learn that we need their side of it
    Or the middle we'll never know

There's no contradiction in marriage
      But it's vital for "cleaving" to be
To have a shift in our thinking
      By re-aligning our loyalty

We don't forget father or mother
      Nor lose sight of the good we're to be
But now all our choices together
      Begin a new line on the family tree

With the passing of years we appreciate
      And learn to adapt and obtain
We become responsible for all our choices
      And the heritage our family now claims

And the love and joy and harmony
      We wanted in our home
Was found by listening to God's word
      And seeking Him alone

The Tied Knot

In looking at the time now claimed
What united two, a tapestry gained
And as one sees the fullness of
An effort woven in tears and love

A sense of beauty and strength adorn
The many intricate patterns formed
And every intersecting strand
Did the test of time withstand

And now the warp and woof of lives
With many colors and textures blend
And interlaced each compliments
The attachment of many woven ends

Each thread alone no beauty lends
Or strength imparts to woven strand
But bound within and firmly strung
It holds impervious to life's demands

And what might two loose ends now claim
Had they not united with one aim
For where once had loomed an empty space
Is a garden where family and friends now grace

Happy 50th Anniversary!

Friends Like Flowers

Friends like flowers cheer the heart

Brighten days when all seems dark

Lighten all our cares and then

Care enough to care again!

At the Lake

The water's cold
The coffee's hot
There's things to do
Right on the spot

There's time to think
To read or play
Where chores are forgotten
For a day

And open hearts
And open arms
Cause hearts to soften
More than charms

And memories link
The days gone past
And lives are touched
By things that last

For life is not all
Fun and games
But caring and seeing
The needed change

And giving our all
And sharing our best
And praying for others
Then letting God do the rest

Blessed Are We

Blest are we to find a friend
      That's closer than a brother
Or one that best describes
      A father or a mother
They hold a place within our heart
      That through advancing years
Remains unchanged except for thoughts
      That only grow far dearer

Someone with a listening ear
      Where we could find a vent
And be a stable source of strength
      Or an encouragement
Who shares our joys as their own
      Someone who really cares
Who at times was more than family
      A gift beyond compare

The Great Divide

Chasms can be formed by tectonic shifting
Or volcanic eruptions or by erosion
A rift begins many separations

A chasm is not a mirror where we see ourselves
It is a reality where one is either on one side
Or the other; we choose to accept or deny reality

We don't necessarily change when we cross a chasm
We choose whether we take *stuff* with us
Or leave it behind; it's our choice

Crossing a chasm requires forward steps
On a definite course, taken with courage
And commitment; only the blind go by their feelings

There are other ways to cross a chasm
Than descending to its depths, but those ways
Are usually man-made; they don't just happen

Imagine

Imagine a plate of favorite fruit
Or one with favorite fresh vegetables
The many varieties of size and shape
And differing colors and textures

Some juicy and sweet
Some crunchy
Each with a different sound, or slurp
And unique flavor

As we munch
Does the apple lose favor
Because it is not a grape
Does the carrot overshadow the beet

Or do we enjoy each one as it is
Letting their differences
Compliment and blend
And satisfy our hunger

Now put a face upon each
A face of a friend
Or family
Or neighbor

There is something in each one
That we can love
Apart from the others
Yet along with the others

Our love for one does not diminish
Our love for the other
Each stands alone, unique
As one with whom our heart can speak

Above the Clouds

Above the clouds the sun shines
    Brightly every day
Above the clouds the storms below
    Are never on display

Above the clouds we're in repose
    Our thoughts are in refrain
Above the clouds though air is thin
    We somehow breathe again

Above the clouds our cares take wing
    And simply fly away
Above the clouds the mountain peaks
    Are within our reach today

Above the clouds we somehow find
    Our bearings once again
Above the clouds we find the strength
    And willingness to descend

Keep Afloat

It's not just any boat
    It's mine
Lots of care gone into it
    At times
Good enough, Yes very good
    It's been
It's carried me oft times
    It's carried friends

Swift upon the water
    Yet sturdy
Wind upon my face
    A little ruddy
Familiar scenes upon the shore
    And tide
Kaleidoscopic memories
    All inside

Dry dock, we all
    Have been
Adjustments and Improvements
    Now and then
But counted on, Yes ready
    When in need
To lift the weight of others
    In good speed

Prepare to sail, though winds may
    Shift again
Have necessary riggings, gear
    And then
Enjoy the work that you have
    Labored in
Godspeed you as each
    Day begins

Happy Birthday

Count the days
Count the years
Count the times between

Add the mercy
Add the grace
Add the victories seen

Multiply the paths we tread
Multiply the friends
Multiply the prayers and strength
      Each to each other lends

Keep the goal ahead in view
Keep the joy alive
Keep the love that God re-news
      Within his love abide

It Hardly Seems Like Yesterday

It hardly seems like yesterday
Though many years have gone
Twas not so very long ago
It seems that you were young

But as you think of times gone by
The working and the fun
May memories you've stored away
Of all the things you've done

Add richness to your storehouse
Of family and friends
And may they be a blessing
As each new day begins

For life is not all looking back
It's today that we must choose
Today we live and sow in hope
It's the time we have to use

We choose to see the rainbow
When it's a cloudy day
We choose to trust that good prevails
As we journey on life's way

We choose to sing a thankful song
We choose again to pray
Then every day that we have lived
Becomes a happy yesterday!

The Old Home Place

Every Home Place has a beginning

But as years go by … It's all about living

It's what goes on within those walls

With family and friends that stop to call

Its prayers and songs and kindness given

It's a refuge and a taste of heaven

It's where the church can gather in

And love can grow and faith begin

And servants, saints and strangers too

Find fellowship and hopes renewed

Yes, things do change throughout the years

There's a sign of aging; some wear and tear

But what's been happening as time's gone on

Is all the living that leaves a song!

Notes in Time

Here's to springtime melodies
    That wake the youthful heart
And yield the golden memories
    That time and years can't part

Here's to the laughter and the fun
    Of golden days in summer's sun
Here's to the strength of faith and friends
    That keeps us till the journey ends

Here's to the love that labors on
    And takes the time to share
By making opportunities
    That lift our woe and care

Here's to autumn's serenade
    That preserves the fruitful part
In all life's vast experiences
    Keeping hope within our heart

Here's to wintertime's refrain
    That thankfulness and gladness bring
When with our hearts we lift in song
    Our vows and prayers again

Here's to the now in every day
    That we with courage live
And keep the melody in our heart
    That God alone can give

Here's to the future days ahead
    When we in chorus blend
The song that all the faithful sing
    Whose God's own son has led

Here's to the joys throughout the years
    And to all your favorite things
And here's a wish that you will have
    All a Happy Birthday brings!

Repairs

A broken cord, a mended string
To keep on working at little things

To learn to laugh and work and play
To listen more closely to what you say

To see how God can change all things
And heal us from the hurts life brings

So we can truly care enough
To bind up broken things with love

To mend the string and broken cord
And find the things we were looking for

The Annual Letter

Each year when the calendar reaches a spot
(It's no date for certain just a feeling mom's got)
But it usually comes as the holidays near
As she puts all on "hold" till her conscience is cleared

The tables are littered with papers and "stuff"
Like address books, envelopes and poems in the rough
Which augment a cycle that sets in motion
All the efforts and will of Mom's devotion

To circulate stories of our family and such
Writing relatives and friends "to just keep in touch"
While old letters and pictures spill on to the floor
The crates full of new ones are piled at the door

The counter top's lined up with inserts to go
Into each bulging envelope stacked in a row
As she hunts for her pen to just add a note
New mail arrives from the folks she just wrote

It's sheer pandemonium as into the night
She works on the piles that seem endless in sight
Dad makes do with "leftovers" found in the fridge
And eats on an armchair a little on edge

As Mom asks again if he wouldn't be able
To just help her out with some mailing labels
But the look of her address book is such a fright
He thinks it's just better to say "good night"

And hope in the morning the coast might be clear
She's done 98, the end's got to be near
One can take only so much 'promoting good cheer'
And be glad it won't happen for another whole year

Good Advice

Oh there's no time like the present, my grandma used to say

A friend in need is a friend indeed, and forgive while it's still day

A stitch in time saves nine. Two wrongs don't make a right

You can catch more flies with honey, and barking dogs won't ever bite

April showers bring May flowers. You'll reap just what you sow

Birds of a feather will flock together. You're responsible for what you know

A penny saved is a penny earned. Remember sunshine follows rain

Every cloud has a silver lining. Sometimes loss is to our best gain

You can lead a horse to water but you cannot make him drink

A word to the wise is sufficient. Do not speak before you think

If nothing's ventured, nothing's gained. Two heads are better than one

Will your practice make you perfect? Jack of all trades or master of none

The early bird usually gets the worm. Early to bed makes it easy to rise

A rolling stone will gather no moss. Make hay while the sun still shines

Absence makes the heart grow fonder. Sometimes out of sight, out of mind

When the cat's away the mice will play. Still waters run deep, you'll find

Don't try to get something for nothing, and practice what you preach

Fools and their money are soon parted. Haste makes waste is what we teach

Cleanliness is next to godliness. Actions speak louder than words

Too many cooks will spoil the broth. Don't wash whites with any colors

All's well that ends well. Better late than never show

Red sky at night is a sailor's delight. Easy come and easy go

Camping Out Of Doors

Our dads helped us pitch the tents out yonder
    With all our dolls and 'stuff' mom wondered
        If there would be room for us
        There was
        And Squiggy and Shadow too

We played all day within forts and castles
Ate supper quick and for once gave no hassle
In getting ready for bed

We loaded up with books and bears
Blankets and flashlights and said "goodnight"
    Without tears
        And trotted off into the night
        Chattering, clattering, without a fight

We settled down again and again
With four bedrolls and two dogs
You do the best that you can

But it was the first of such occasion
And it took each of us
        Much persuasion
        From each other
        That night would soon pass

But Oooh it was an awful fright
To be out late and out of sight
The darkness crept around us all

And fears of goblins made their call
And groans and moans from upper windows
        Made us shriek and grab our sandals
        Running out the nearest gate
        To go back home before too late

And we never heard Ginny laugh!

Baking Time

Before the counter top we all
Lined up on steps and stools
Our aprons on and hair tied back
Hands washed it was the rule

With neighbor kids we all would watch
As mom would hand each one
A spoon or measuring cup or bowl
Our task had now begun

The eggs were cracked and shells fished out
The sugar was licked and stirred
And every kind of condiment
Was added if we could

She never made us frosting
We never could understand
She said the dough was sweet enough
As she washed our sticky hands

With all the bowls of goodies
That we had sprinkled on the top
Each cookie was a masterpiece
Of ingenuity and thought

The waiting was the hardest part
But finally pan by pan
Was taken from the oven to
The table where we would stand

And before we could even take a bite
Though it was never really planned
We had to count all the red hots
On the cookies held in our hand!

Quality Time with Dad

Chapter books and chapter time
Feeding squirrels at the park
Day off ties, motorbike rides
Quality naps with the dog
Four square, combing hair
'Rounds' at AGH
Never 'On Call' when we're havin fun
Never 'On Call' when it hurts
Coffee breaks, fishin at lakes
French toast on Saturday Morn
Watchin swim meets, doing bicycle feats
Playing *Solid Rock* or the *Charlie Brown* song
Igloos each spring, eating donut rings
Music camp, playing ball and other things
Groaning at jokes; hearing about folks
Like Leonard and Mary Jane B.
Tying knots, fixing cuckoo clocks
Oil changes with the plug in the pan
Shootin at the range
Thinking dad's a bit strange
Asking for 'Herb' at the Pizza Hut
Learning to drive in Montana with five
"We're Wandler's, that's our dad over there"
Learning math loudly, fixing computers partly
E-mailing to keep college kids closer
Seeing there were boys, he added to the toys
Started baking plachinda and strudel
You might think dad was always there
With all our books and pictures
But it's a quantitative thing
That only years can measure

Wheels for All Seasons

The wheel was undoubtedly a most important invention
Where we'd be without it is beyond comprehension
For to chart one's life from its earliest years
Finds us rolling on whatever prevails with our peers

There are new wheels and old wheels, some smoking, some hot
There's clean wheels and broken wheels, some borrowed, some bought
Some have budding new bikers; some bikers are not
And when accidents happen, they're mostly forgot

Some wheels behind bikers aren't bikes for a reason
There are all kinds of bikers and wheels for all seasons
There are bikes that are licensed, and bikers that aren't
There are wheels for the young and those young at heart

There are wheels for school busses and fire trucks for school
There's riders that act and think they are cool
There are changes of wheels, but mostly wheels with tire changes
There are old farts with no wheels spending time at firing ranges

There's *wanna*-be bikers and bikes on the run
There's training wheels, bygone wheels and wheels just for fun
There are wheels just for campers and campers on wheels
When dad escorts musicians playing musical chairs

But whether it's long rides or short rides in sun or bad weather
Whether its Harley riders, girly riders, nephew riders or whatever
There's one thing for certain if there's ever a voice
It will be hill over dale and the hills get first choice

127

The Reader

The court would assemble at bed time hour
As *The Reader* would call from his lair
And his subjects would clamor and climb all about
Till settled in the old arm chair

Then carefully claiming a 'chapter book'
From childhood collections of old
The Reader, three kids (and their dog) would be
Transported by tales that were told

There were Ooohs! and Aaahs! and cries of delight
And some pummeling over mean Danny Rugg
And tears for many a poor doggie's plight
And laughter again for his pluck

From thick Highland brogue of wee lads and lassies
To Cossack, Hun, villains and such
The booming voice of *The Reader* transformed
Every character with variations of Deutsch

And with desire for keeping his children alert
And fine-tuning their listening skills
He would now and then adlib just a bit
Amidst insults and cries of appeal

Kids and dog now sprawled themselves by the fire
New interests sparked reader and crew
As trilogies of Hobbits and star war knights
And serial novels now grew

The Age of *The Reader* and listeners reversed
As college and jobs now resumed
And stories enjoyed on trips far and near
Were written, rehearsed and exhumed

And now *The Reader* still sits by the fire
Examining old stories and new
And he sometimes reads aloud to his wife
And sometimes he'll listen and muse.

Some memories grow old with the passing of years
Some fade for lack of review
Some donned with embellishment become more refined
Some are legends because of their use

If Only

If only our little transgressions in life

Were matters of greater concern

We'd avoid much recrimination and strife

If sooner than later we'd learn

For sooner than later we'd make some amend

If sooner our conscience were pricked

By our careless, thoughtless or hasty mistakes

That simply turn into regrets

For deeds and words later we wished were undone

Must needs bring forgiveness to bear

And sooner or later return in our thoughts

To remind us our need in prayer

Lists

There was a list made out for me
Of chores to do after school
It was added to the homework list
My teachers gave as a rule

And mother always had a list
While packing for any vacation
Counting all our socks and things
Was part of our education

Then came the lists of many rules
Applied to every occasion
And often amended as time went by
To counter any omission

At work it wasn't much better
As graphs and charts were used
To list each success or failure
Depending on who got to choose

But now that I am my own boss
You'd think things would be great
For anything I need at all
I could just delegate

For all the things that I must do
Are simply at my request
But I find it quite a task to think
That I must make out the list!

The Mirror Image

As I look into the mirror
What is it that I see
Do I really know the person
That's looking back at me

Or would it come as a surprise
The reverse is now before my eyes
And what I think is true of me
May not be quite what others see

Though images may seem the same
And answer to a common name
A subtle difference yet is there
That seldom causes thought or care

Unless, of course, we see in others
Things they never see
And it pricks our conscience slightly
Could that be true of me?

Yet there is still a better way
Than what we think or others say
To see with greater clarity
Our life and who we are

For no one knows us better
Than our Father up above
Who desires we bear the image
Of His son, whom we would love

My Future

Were all my yesterdays worthwhile
With all the training and the trial
Will I keep in mind and heart the things
That from my youth a standard rings
And if performed a blessing brings

Or will it all be laid aside
As world philosophies arise
And man's ideas seek to steal
The very thoughts
That once were real

The very life I wished to live
And promises that in this give
Will I seek to prove them days ahead
With what my mind and heart are fed
Depending on which book I've read

Depending on the friends I keep
Depending on how much I seek
Will I follow vanity and try
To be like others passing by
Debating worldly, selfish lies

Life poses questions never thought
Imagination now is sought
But as today we live and choose
May it be balanced by the truth
Of honest things we learned in youth

May straight the arrow meet its mark
Value all that's kept within the ark
And look to a future bright and see
The very person I could be
By grasping all God planned for me

Another Year

Another year ahead of you
    Another year behind
So many things to think and do
    So much may cross your mind
But as each day begins anew
    And as each day will end
Be true to all you know is true
    Be true to your <u>best</u> friend
Look not at just the day ahead
    Look up and look beyond
There is a path that leads to peace
    There's a treasure to be found

Our View

Our view of things is different
   Depending on where we stand
Our difference in perspective too
   May change, with change of hands
What today is very near to us
   In attitude and charm
Will often lose intensity
   As time continues on
And soon positions others take
   And our freedom to explore
Will open up more options
   Of opinions, facts and more
And soon we'll find, as others have
   Such confusion in the mix
There's little hope of consensus
   On any topic fixed
   ~ Then ~
It's time to stop and consider
   The ground we're standing on
It's time to look much higher
   Than the views we find around
It's time to look ahead of us
   Just where our end will be
It's time to trace our roots again
   And see just where they lead
Our present stance, our future days
   Are much clearer from God's view
For there's dirt and there is Holy ground
   There's fantasy; there's truth
There's a natural end to everything
   There's eternity in view
And the faith begotten in our life
   Will affect the things we choose

Today

As each new day begins
      And as the hours pass
As choices, thoughts would claim
      Your focus, time or task
Remember that *today*
      Others hold you in their heart
No strings attach their care and love
      No motives to cast doubt
Tho far away, tho oft unseen
      Yet unmoved by life's dismays
Today they can be reached by you
      They are your friends always

Count Today

Our life is but a little while
    Our days but numbered hours
And though we count them year by year
    Their measure is beyond our powers

Each breath we take and morning new
    Each opportunity
Is an investment with returns
    Or cash in hand that flees

So consider all your goals ahead
    The many possibilities
But most important count today
    It directs your destiny

Consider early in the day
    First thing, when you get up
And get the guidance and the help
    To cope when things disrupt

For it's today that really counts
    The next step leads the way
Put forth your greatest effort
    While it is called today

Quote of the year:
My dad says, "Nothin' but the best for my kids."

The deciding factor when Beth chose her computer modem. (Of course Bruce made that statement at the grocery store while trying to decide between skim milk and 2%!)

College Life

The kids were gone, the dog was dead
That's the beginning, they say, of your best years ahead

But the feeling of calm was fleeting at best
After last year's fast lane, we're now on *express*

With the summer filled with so many excursions
All three left in such haste, it was utter confusion

People asked if we missed them, but there was nothing to fear
If you looked in their rooms, you'd think they're still here

The empty nest syndrome was a myth in disguise
We've hardly had time to dry the tears from our eyes

With four trips to *Whitman* and three to WAZZU
And dinners with Ginny as we're passing through

Juggling phone machines, faxes and computer modems
Wondering why our phone bill's still high since the e-mail explosion

And we'd almost lost count of which one we'd see next
When Thanksgiving arrived and so did their guests

But we haven't forgotten we'd planned to relax
And finish some projects put off in the past

Or read a book by a cozy fire, eat a bonbon or two if we so desire
It will just have to wait until the New Year

I guess that's enough comfort to give us some cheer

Twins Abroad

We thought their plans had all been made
They were settled as could be
Until the phone began to ring
(Things come in pairs, you see)

    Bad News! They've dropped my program, Mom
    My plans have all been wrecked
    But no problem, for I've transferred schools
    I'll just need another check

I hardly had time to turn around
Was barely out the door
When her sister called to break the news
Australia's not her choice any more

    So now instead of Mexico
    One's Costa Rica bound
    And Zimbabwe must be somewhere
    Among all the maps I've found

One wonders how to do without
Six months will be quite a trial
But with all the lists, three bags were packed
A lesson in self-denial

    Oh there was agonization and consternation
    With logical suggestions abused
    Every configuration for relocation
    And imagination for solutions were used

But with complications and trepidations
There was consolation too
As their visitations and salutations and socialization grew
Departations met with exultation that only their family knew

We were just enough deluded
Thinking things would now go right
There's not much worse could happen
After the first one missed her flight

But Mother Nature intervenes
When least we would expect
The other left in a blizzard
We never will forget

We can span the globe in seconds with e-mail, fax and phone
But when the world is at their feet and your kids begin to roam
The far away…seems far away, as snails and postcards travel
The patience of the stout in heart, even begins to unravel
But now the maps are on the wall and books are near at hand
We've lifted our horizons, new adventures we have planned
Because our kids have opened up the world for us to see
We're now connected to distant shores; we never thought we'd be

Long Ago

Long ago in a far away land
There were three little girls
One more than was planned

But friends pitched right in
Crocheted blankets galore, to
Bundle them up for trips out the door

Then as the years passed there were
Birthday cakes too, and parties with
Presents, and laughs quite a few

With friends that took care of so many
Arrangements; it kept mom, dad and kids
Quite full of engagements

But alas, they grew up and married
One day. Three handsome princes
Just carried them away

But before they all left
There was still much 'a do'
As all these friends gathered in unison to

Share once again all their love and good will
And for this little family
It's been more than a thrill

The Rose

Climbing, creeping and rambling about
Rich graceful blossoms clustered throughout
Sending sweet fragrance from trellis and bower
The rose in bloom is a beautiful flower

Red ones for love, optimistic and bright
Yellow encourages, with cheer and delight
Pink soft and tender, the passion of youth
White speaks of purity, promise and truth

So may a bouquet of roses for you
Be a reminder of vows between two
And may sweet memories cascade today
Like roses the summer of your wedding day

Getting Ready

Mom's out washing fence posts, there's rose bushes in the hall
Dad just wants some supper, he's been working after all

It seems Mom's gone to the grocers a dozen times this week
She's got food stored around everywhere, but there's nothing we can eat

Mom's been working in the kitchen and Dad's supposed to clean the garage
He's moved the bikes and the Harley, now he's swept up in his entourage

Mom's back out in the garden, making war with a family of moles
They've uprooted all her geraniums and made the yard a pocket of holes

So Dad's busy settin a trap line, but when he stops to clean his 44
He decides to take the boys shootin, with ammo enough for any war

Mom says she needs a new Frigidaire, says she'll put it out in the shed
Dad just calmly folds the paper, says he thinks it's time for bed

He's getting a bit suspicious that something's going on around here
Beth says he needs a tuxedo and to forget the STP this year

And he's worried that those tux tails, won't fit the Harley seat just right
But Mom says not to worry, because the BBQ's here tomorrow night

There's only two things on his "to do" list, so he shouldn't look so forlorn
Just remember to get the U-Haul, for the roses on Saturday morn

Now Dad's talking on the telephone, seems he's starting to get things clear
He remembers taking a few days off, for a weddin going on around here

144

The Wedding

Surrounded by friends, the joy of the day
Amidst all the vows, the hopes that they raise

Among all the gifts, the wishes, the sup
A mother drew near with an empty cup

Carried by servants, something to share
Wine that sustains us, because Jesus cares

All that can gladden the heart without fear
Help meet each experience with hope and cheer

So after the joys of this day are gone
The songs of rejoicing may continue on

Grandchildren

We're blessed with many grandchildren
Our grandpa and grandma say

They love to have us come and visit
When we can stay and play

With puzzles and toys from many years ago
And bicycle rides with grandpa, you know

The cousins come from miles around
Where sharing is learned and smiles abound

And just like flavors of ice cream cones
They can't decide their favorite one

So with cookies and treats we're spoiled as can be
Because we're their favorite ones, you see

And when it's time to say good-bye
There are hugs and kisses and sometimes we cry

But our moms are sure as we drive away
The ones loved best, were the ones with them today

Yes, grandpa and grandma love us everyone
We're all their favorite grandchildren

Aunt Hilda Comes Just Once a Year

Aunt Hilda comes just once a year
    A week at most, but don't you fear

For every day the project list
    Stretches so, she just can't rest

We try to schedule things by days
    But looking back it's just a haze

Of baking cookies and baking bread
    Or making cinnamon rolls instead

Then there's other things to do
    Like sewing PJ's … quite a few

Or having concerts: "tickets please"
    Or smiling for more pictures: "Cheese!"

The grand finale always is
    "Plachinda Day" with all the kids

And many hands with floured faces
    Really puts one through the paces

And though the new Bosch mixer sped
    Assembly lines were still ahead

The coffee breaks were near at hand
    And sugar highs around the bend

But all good things come to an end
    It's Ibuprofen and to bed

For Aunt Hilda comes but once a year
    And a week may be too much, we fear

Time with Grandpa

Some grandpas take you fishing
Some play ball in the yard
Some give you rides on a tractor
Or play miniature golf at the park

Some grandpas watch you play soccer
Some may visit your school
Some may like to tell stories
Or let you tinker with their tools

Some grandpas may call you each Sunday
Some may live very near
Some may plan special occasions
When you see them just once in a year

Now I have a grandpa that rides bikes
He has bicycles, not a few
And his most fun times are planning
All the bike rides his grandkids will do

At first we bicycled around the block
Then it was down the lane
And before too long we were all on the trail
Called by some, "The Interurban"

We've ridden on treks from the ferry
We've ridden to Marymoor Park
We've ridden uphill to the Dairy Queen
Where our bikes filled the parking lot

It's nice when there's sunshiny weather
It's nice when the sky is clear
But sometimes it's wet and chilly
And we have to put on our rain gear

We've learned a few things from grandpa
Like sometimes the ride is uphill
And sometimes you need to stop for a break
Or wait for the group to appear

Grandpa likes to make every challenge
Something we can say that we've done
And though the miles keep adding up
With the effort, there's always some fun

It's fun to do stuff with my grandpa
But sometimes he has funny rules
Like we can't pass him going up a hill
And it's grape or gripe jelly we use

149

Fishing at Grandma's

It's time to put the curtain up
It's time to find the gear
It's time again for fishing
At grandma's house this year

It takes a lot of planning
Asking questions, quite a few
Like what the kids are needing
Or maybe wanting too

Not many grandkids do as we
Fishing for presents without a tree
But stand in lines with fishing poles
Casting and straining while grandpa pulls

He has some helpers behind the screen
It's usually Allen and Eileen
Who fill the snowman bags each time
A line is cast and a name is chimed

And if the present just won't fit
It's a bottom fish that must have bit
And underneath the cloth it goes
Retrieved by hands instead of poles

It's really a wonder to big and small
How grandma's idea started at all
But doing it once made it a tradition
Everyone wants the fishing expedition

Pumpkin Pocket Pies
a.k.a. Plachinda Day

Oh my goodness
Extra kids!
Who brought rolling pins?
Where's the sugar lid?

There's 9 of us, grandpa
We need more dough!
We can bake a few more
Before we have to go.

Elbows all are touching
Bowls go here and back
Is this how you do it?
Does it matter if it's patched?

You need to pinch and poke it
Cuz it steams and that's a fact
I think I've got it now
Let me put it on the rack!

Aunt Ginny's busy baking
Grandpa makes the dough
Aunt Porsche at the island
Keeps the workforce all in tow

Aunt Beth is supervising
Grandma's bringing lunch
Krista circles once again
With pointers for the bunch

The quality control
Is ignored another year
But grandpa's satisfied
That his grandkids are all here

It truly is amazing
Once the baking is all done
It really is quite tasty
Congratulations everyone!

Today is Mine
(A song of hope)

Today is mine and I would see
The gifts that God would give to me
I'll take His hand so I can be
Led in the path He's planned for me
To victor be

Today is mine and I would know
How much through faith God will bestow
I'll give my life for Him to mold
And in Christ's likeness there behold
His love for me

Today is mine and I will pray
I'll hear each word that God will say
I know He cares, I will obey
He's planned each step along the way
That's best for me

Today is mine, my choice will be
To see the Christ on Calvary
I realize that I'd be there
Instead His resurrected life I share
He died for me

Today is mine, God's gift to me
I'll love and serve Him joyfully
I'll walk with Jesus faithfully
And trust God's promises to me
His child I'll be

Family

F fantastic forbearing funny fearless fostering funded familiar festive frictional frustrating faithful friendly feeling flexible filial father feeding

A acknowledged affectionate assuring approachable abiding articulating active accountable accumulative accomplished accommodating

M matrimonial merry medicinal migratory maternal melodramatic mannerly mundane merciful metamorphic memorable mother

I imposing imperfect interdependent international imaginative interested idiomatic ideologic instructed integrated identity

L loving living learning listening lodgings labor loyal lively lasting lucky leisure laughing lavish label

Y yarns youngsters yummies yammering yokefellow yielding yapping youthful yearning yes you

Author Bios

For many years Donna has enjoyed sharing her poems with family and friends. Her writings often depict the simple pleasures of life and the lessons of life. Her Norwegian grandmother, a poet and prodigious letter writer, helped influence expressing her faith in this manner. She credits her husband, Bruce, for introducing many events that became family traditions. Donna is a homemaker with a teaching degree. She resides with her husband, a retired surgeon, in Auburn, WA. Their three married daughters and families live in the Puget Sound area.

Her mailing address is P.O. Box 1692, Auburn, WA 98071

155

Made in the USA
San Bernardino, CA
26 March 2015